Nijinsky: Death of a Faun

on the apres-matin
- many thanks for
all the pleasure you've
gine me during
this play between us

David.

First published in 1996 by Oberon Books Ltd (incorporating Absolute Classics), 521 Caledonian Road, London N7 9RH. Tel: 0171 607 3637/Fax: 0171 607 3629

ISBN 1 84002 000 8

Cover design: Andrzej Klimowski

Cover typography: Richard Doust

Printed by Arrowhead Ltd, Limited, Reading

David Pownall

NIJINSKY
DEATH OF A FAUN

Oberon Books
London

For J. J. and John Adler

Nicholas Johnson as Nijinsky

INTRODUCTION

Coming from a musical family, although he studied law in St Petersburg, Sergei Diaghilev (1872-1929) also studied music during a remarkably creative period in Russia. He became an influential member of a circle of artists, including Benois, Vakst, Nouvel, with whom he founded in 1899 Mir Iskousstva, a magazine devoted to the arts which had a short but influential life until 1904. It may seem paradoxical to talk of Diaghilev as a revolutionary when he took little part in the political ferment around him in his impressionable years. As an intelligent man he was aware of the pressures and divisions which led his country to a series of major political and social upheavals, ending in the Communist revolution. Yet he devoted his life to fostering a series of intellectual upheavals in the arts, a revolutionary in the purist sense, making fewer compromises and accepting fewer restraints. Where Lenin and communist ideology could never subsequently come to terms with the role of the arts and of the artist, other than as useful propaganda, subservient to the social and political interests of the state, Diaghilev's career came closer to exemplifying Shelley's bold claim that poets—creative artists—were the "unacknowledged legislators of mankind".

He was a man of scholarship and taste, with a flair for detecting and responding to the talents of others, but lacked a creative impulse himself in any of the arts he cared so much about. Yet his determination to bring artists together and make things happen can only be seen and understood as a series of creative acts. His first triumph was in arranging an influential exhibition of Russian paintings, opening the eyes of his Russian contemporaries to their own cultural achievement. Understandably he was attracted to the Opera House, which itself represented a combination of the arts which most interested him, music and painting, spectacle and drama; and his interest in ballet was possibly enhanced by his homosexuality, since the Russian Ballet had maintained the importance of the male dancer, and attractive, classically proportioned and supremely healthy young men were very much on display. He certainly began an affair with the most talented of them, Vaslav Nijinsky.

Diaghilev's attempts to work within the Imperial Theatre, first as editor of their year book, and then with responsibility for a production of *Sylvia* ended in disagreement and official disgrace. He then presented in 1906 in Paris an exhibition of Russian painting, in 1907 a season of Russian music and in 1908 a brief season of Russian opera, followed in 1909 by a longer season of Russian opera and ballet. With the overwhelming success of the ballet in 1909 he finally found his metier. European ballet for decades before Diaghilev had been a popular but artistically negligible entertainment. Diaghilev had the advantage of bringing back to the rest of Europe from Russia, something that European ballet had lost, the importance of male dancing, the excitement of pas de deux and of ensemble dancing where women and men participated as equal partners. His first programme included the Polovstian dances from *Prince Igor*, and the ferocity and virile display of the male dancing was quite outside the dance experience of his French audience, so that Diaghilev had an immediate success. The concept too which his artistic advisers had hammered out in discussion, of an equal partnership between theme, choreography, design and music made just as much impact, and in particular the designs of Bakst had a revolutionary effect in fashion on clothes, interior decoration, textiles and graphics.

The first night at the Theatre du Chatelet, 18th May 1909, with Tamara Karsavina, Bronislava Nijinska, Michel Fokine, Adolph Bolm, Vaslav Nijinsky, Mikhail Mordkin and Laurent Novikov ushered in a revolution, not only in western theatre, but particularly in theatre dance. By then ballet outside Russia had degenerated into mere spectacle, with long ballets of many acts, with the plot an excuse rather than a reason for the display of over-decorated and bejewelled ballerinas, involved in make-believe love affairs with other female dancers dressed en travesti as men, against a background of simple routines danced by pink-shoed corps de ballet, amply proportioned in most of the right places, wearing conventional tutus to reveal most of what they had. In contrast, Diaghilev's one-act ballets combined costumes, decor, music, lighting, dancing and dramatic action into a closely knit and carefully integrated whole. In addition there was the extraordinary impact of his leading male dancer, Vaslav Nijinsky, who captivated everybody's imagination with his rare gift for not only seeming to become the roles he was playing on stage but able to project these in all there complexity to their dazzled audience. At the same time Nijinsky astonished with virtuoso, bravura steps, seeming to hang in the air at the top of his formidable jumps, and effortlessly keep the perfect line of the well trained dancer so that trunk and limbs maintained the balance and proportions in movement that are the basis of classical ballet. It is difficult for us to recapture the overwhelming effect of these changes on an otherwise sophisticated audience.

Diaghilev however was not interested in popularity as such, much less box office success, although he obviously welcomed them when they arrived. He was interested in what was going on in the fine arts, particularly music, painting, sculpture and literature. From 1909 he presided over what became his own ballet company (presented as the Ballets Russes de Serge Diaghilev from 1911), which toured Europe with considerable prestige among an influential upper middle class and aristocratic public, the opera house audience of his day. He increasingly came to act as a channel between developments in the fine arts and a discriminating public, trusted by creative artists who admired his judgements and achievements and increasingly by his public who relied on his taste and discrimination to introduce them to what was valuable in the artistic developments of the time.

The two decades, the 1910's and 20's, of his reign, happened to be periods of intense and widespread change in the arts at perhaps the last time when there was a general view that developments in the fine arts mattered and were important.

In mediating between artists and public, Diaghilev played an invaluable role, and by bringing such artists together, gave the art of ballet prestige and an importance which transcended even its finest achievements in its romantic heyday in the 1840's. Then, as almost the last art form to respond to the romantic movement, in the creative hands of Perrot it caught the essence of that artistic revolution.

It was not just that distinguished artists like Picasso and Stravinsky worked in the Diaghilev ballet, but that they first found their public through the ballet. Occasionally as in the furore over *The Rite of Spring* or the failure of *Les Noces*, Diaghilev went well beyond his public, but particularly with *The Rite of Spring* in 1913 the public soon came to realise how wrong they had been in disliking it, and this helped to increase Diaghilev's prestige. In the process he gave ballet an unprecedented boost as an art form, so that everywhere students, intelligent and gifted students started studying dance and ballet's audience increased as the fuss in upper middle class and aristocratic circles filtered through the media until more and more middle class audiences started going to ballet.

When Diaghilev's company broke up at his death, he had created a growing public demand for ballet which his less respectable artistic successors happily cashed in on. Until well into the 1950's there was also a public conviction that the only *real* ballet was Russian, another of Diaghilev's achievements, however much his designers and composers were French and however many of his dancers were English with false names.

Recently a media view of Diaghilev as an outrageously obvious homosexual, using his company as a private male brothel, has been projected. It is historically false. When Nijinsky married and Diaghilev expelled him from the company, Diaghilev began a close relationship with the young Massine who, in his old age, publicly regretted leaving Diaghilev early in his career since the influence of Diaghilev's knowledge and discernment had been equivalent to "spending time very pleasantly with the finest teacher at the best university".

Diaghilev was greatly respected by his company and his artistic associates. Most of the rows and feuds and bitter acrimony, and there were plenty of them, were over artistic questions not scandalous ones. Even when they disagreed with him, people obviously respected his judgement. Sir Anton Dolin has remembered Diaghilev coming to the rehearsal of a pas de deux Massine had made and demanding changes, which were provided without question. How many modern choreographers would change a key *pas de deux* at the behest of their company director? On his unexpected death in 1929, Diaghilev's company broke up. Some of the repertory and some of the dancers later to be brought back together by Colonel de Basil. Early works for his company included *Les Sylphides, Scheherazade, Carnaval, Firebird, Petrouchka, Le Spectre de la Rose, L'Après Midi d'un Faune* and *The Rite of Spring*. During the 1914/18 war when many dancers were unable to leave Russia, Diaghilev used Nemchinova, Sokolova (born Hilda Munnings the first English ballerina to appear with the company), Woizikowsky, Idzikovsky and later Olga Spessivsteva. After the war French influence became prominent in design and music with Picasso, Matisse, Derain, Laurencin, Poulenc, Auric and Satie; Fokine and Nijinsky were succeeded as choreographers by Massine, Nijinska and Balanchine. In 1921, as a tribute to imperial Russia's golden ballet past, Diaghilev revived *The Sleeping Beauty* in London, and although it proved a financial failure, it had a striking influence on a number of those who saw it, including Ninette de Valois. But by then Vaslav Nijinsky had for many years been incarcerated in a lunatic asylum.

Vaslav Nijinsky, born in Kiev in 1888, is with the possible exception of Rudolph Nureyev, generally regarded as the greatest male dancer of the twentieth century. His affair with Diaghilev added a particular frisson of sensation and scandal to what was anyway an amazing reputation as a performance artist. He was trained at the Russian Imperial Ballet School in St. Petersburg, early showing an innate ability for classical ballet and a good ear for music. He played, more by ear than by sight-reading, the piano, the flute, the balalaika and the accordion. He first appeared in public as a dancer at the age of 18 and soon partnered the leading ballerinas as a member of the Imperial Russian Ballet, Khchessinska, Preobajenska, Pavlova and Karsavina. He appeared in Diaghilev's first successful season of ballet in Paris in 1909, and in 1911 he left the Imperial company for good intending to be with Diaghilev on a permanent basis.

By then they were lovers. Nijinsky had been seduced by Prince Pavel Dmitrievitch Lvov who after a few months handed him on to Count Tishkievitch, who in turn introduced him to Diaghilev. Affairs between men, particularly between good-looking young men and older men, were accepted as part of the social scene in St. Petersburg in a way they were not, if we are to believe Proust, in Paris and certainly not in London, if we are to judge by the sad example of Oscar Wilde and Lord Alfred Douglas a decade earlier. Diaghilev neither flaunted nor made a secret of his homosexuality, and this was viewed in London as being shocking but acceptable as part of his being "a foreigner". All the same his affair with Nijinsky was to help in leaving an indelible prejudice in the public's view of the male ballet dancer, which in the 1960's Nureyev's similar sexual bias was only to reinforce.

This was not all. In the 1900's, one of the few areas where it was possible to view scantily clad young males flaunting their masculine beauty in an aura of artistic respectability was the ballet. Inevitably this attracted a particular segment of the audience, as much for erotic as for artistic satisfaction. They were there as much because they were wallowing in a fantasy love affair with a particular dancer, as because they admired the decor, the music or the choreography. This introduced a hothouse atmosphere into opera house ballet audiences, which in many ways again reinforced prejudice against ballet in general. Even with the popularity of ballet in the 1960's, with queues for Fonteyn and Nureyev performances stretching all round Covent Garden Opera House all night, this element in the audience remained noticeable. Only since the spread of disco dancing in the 70's, particularly now when so many young men, wearing almost nothing, dance the night away, crammed in an athletic sprawl, everybody showing off as well as admiring each other, has the particular appeal of ballet waned, and the ballet audience changed. Nowadays those who want to watch athletic young men wearing little and showing off their good looks in dance, go to the nearest disco, where ecstasy of various kinds is all too readily available. The modern ballet audience goes to the theatre for more artistically respectable reasons.

In his heyday Nijinsky must have been the focus for a good many of those fantasy love affairs. Not only women in the audience, but a proportion of the men in the audience too would appear to have been quite wildly excited by his performances. There was an almost palpable air of tension and excitement when he appeared on stage, an almost audible increase in heavy breathing in the stalls. One of the women in his audience in 1912 was to have an astonishing effect on his life. Her name was Romola de Pulska.

In 1911 for Diaghilev, Nijinsky choreographed *L'Après Midi d'un Faune* which ended in uproar and was a *succès de scandale.* Even more uproar was caused by his choreography in 1913 for *The Rite of Spring*, although his *Jeux*, made in the same year, was better received. But in 1913 things had changed.

Diaghilev, having been told by a fortune teller that he would die on water, refused to travel by sea, and sent his company off on their own for an American tour. (Ironically he died in Venice). On the boat Nijinsky became engaged to a Hungarian dancer with the company whose language he did not understand while she did not understand his. Her name was Romola de Pulska. When Diaghilev heard what had happened Nijinsky was immediately dismissed. Why did Nijinsky do it? Diaghilev's rage is very understandable. "Hell hath no fury" et cetera. For Nijinsky we have to be more understanding. He was alone, night after night on board a cruise ship for three weeks. He was twenty-four, with a pretty girl throwing herself at him. He was a young romantic male, with little or no experience of everyday life apart from the rarified atmosphere of ballet school and ballet theatre, wanting to be a man like other men, wanting to be a father, to have children, wanting to be that most romantic illusion of all for those whose brilliant creative talents inevitably make them feel different from their fellows, wanting to be normal. Ironically Nijinsky had been well brought up. For a romantic idealist, an affair would not do. He had to go the whole hog and get married.

Whom had he fallen for? What lay behind the determined lines of that pretty face? Romola de Pulska was not really a dancer. She was in the words of Nijinsky's sister" a socialite". She professed to want to learn ballet in order to be allowed to become a lowly member of the Diaghilev company, because she was obsessed with Nijinsky. Her maid occupied the accommodation allocated to Romola on board ship for South America. She herself purchased a first class ticket which allowed her to mix not only with the important members of the company also travelling first class, but with Nijinsky himself. Nijinsky did not inform Diaghilev of his intention to marry. Diaghilev read of it in the newspapers. Nijinsky did not inform his mother, nor his sister either, although he was devoted to both of them. Years later Romola said to Nijinsky's sister "I am not stupid as to give advanced notice of our wedding plans to Diaghilev or to Vaslav's family and risk your stopping us."

These words reveal a great deal. They make it depressingly clear that Nijinsky was exchanging the domination of Diaghilev for the domination of a scheming, manipulative woman. Diaghilev's devotion had led to world fame and the challenge of creativity, of making new ballets as well as dancing demanding roles. Romola's domination led to mental instability and finally madness.

Romola Flavia Nijinsky, Countess de Pulska Luboc and Cselfalva, was the granddaughter of one of the instigators of the Hungarian revolution of 1848 who was given asylum in England, and whose children were born and brought up in England. So Romola was British by birth. Her father

Charles de Pulski, one of the founders of the Hungarian National Gallery, had her educated in France and England, and since her mother was a leading Hungarian actress, Romola studied drama in Paris. After idolising Nijinsky, seen in performance in 1912, she studied dance with Enrico Cecchetti and joined the Diaghilev company in 1913.

Romola's version of her life with Nijinsky, seen almost entirely from her point of view and seldom questioning the rightness of her decisions much less her motives, has largely held the field. In 1933, while Nijinsky was a mental patient, she published *Nijinsky* which became a bestseller and was translated into sixteen languages. She later published *Last Years of Nijinsky* and edited *The Diary of Vaslav Nijinsky*. The world's view of Nijinsky has been seen very much through her eyes. Yet for anyone viewing the facts and events dispassionately, a rather different picture must emerge.

Nijinsky had appalling luck. There is something akin to ancient Greek tragedy in the way this supremely gifted creative artist was ground down by events he could not control. Expelled from the Diaghilev company, he briefly attempted to form his own but this ended in disaster in London, where he caught influenza and was seriously ill for two months. He was then caught in Budapest by the outbreak of World War I and confined to house arrest as an enemy alien. This lasted from 1914 to 1916. Unable to dance, much less create ballets, he was cooped up with a domineering, opinionated wife and her mother and step-father. Romola did not get on with her mother who felt she should divorce Nijinsky. It is sad to imagine the effect this backbiting and feuding atmosphere must have had on a sensitive and imaginative artist.

There are two versions of schizophrenia. One school holds that its origins lie in some physical deficiency. The school of R D Laing has on the contrary held that retreat into madness can be induced as the only escape from the impossible double binds and emotional tangles in which members of a family inflict terrible, even if sometimes unintentional, traumas on each other. His time in Budapest, away from everyone he knew, deprived entirely of the one world, classical ballet, where he was so pre-eminent, at the mercy of relatives whose language he did not even understand, not to mention a wife convinced of the rightness of everything she did, could not be more stressful. It is tempting to see this unhappy time as being the inevitable cause of Nijinsky's slow slide into incapacity and madness.

In 1916 he was rescued from this terrifying milieu and asked by Diaghilev to head his company in a tour of America, not only as its principal dancer but temporarily in charge of the artistic direction of the company. Diaghilev did not of course accompany them, and Nijinsky's name was needed to make the tour a success. The company included Leonid Massine who had succeeded him not only as a young star, not only as a potential choreographer, but also in Diaghilev's bed. On the tour the two of them alternated the leading role in *Petrouchka* where an elderly puppet master manipulates his doll-like figures who prove to have all too human emotions. The puppet Petrouchka was a role in which Nijinsky excelled. A role for which he was in some ways, almost typecast. His wife came with him on the tour, scenting plots and hidden strategies on all sides. Herself so devious, she ascribed base motives to almost everybody's actions. The stress and strain on Nijinsky, particularly as he was creating what would prove to be his last ballet *Till Eulenspiegel*, coming on top of his long confinement in Budapest, must have been almost unendurable. Then when Nijinsky joined the Diaghilev company in Madrid again, and Diaghilev seemed willing to forgive and forget, his wife still saw plots and intrigues at every turn and persuaded Nijinsky into such impossible behaviour that the break with Diaghilev became final. Nijinsky's last public performance was in Buenos Aires where he stayed on to give a gala performance after his final appearance with the Diaghilev ballet there in *Le Spectre de la Rose* and *Petrouchka*. The following year he was diagnosed as insane and, through the wilful behaviour of his mother-in-law and her husband, confined to a state asylum where his brutal treatment reduced him to a catatonic state. He was never fully to recover, and died after periods in and out of asylums and nursing homes, in 1950.

David Pownall's play envisages him in one of his more sympathetic institutions in 1929, learning of the death of Diaghilev. It gives us a rare and perceptive insight into the working of Nijinsky's mind as he looks back over the horrifying events of his life. The play was a success at the 1991 Edinburgh International Festival and in 1992 at the Tel Aviv, Bournemouth and Chichester Festivals. In 1993 the play did well in London at the Orange Tree Theatre and in Berlin at the Deutsche Oper. In 1995 it was sent by the British Council on an extensive tour of Scandinavia and the Netherlands. In 1996 after further success at the Brisbane Festival it was invited to a return engagement in Australia and 1997 sees its American premiere in New York.

Nijinsky was only 29 when he gave up dancing, and there can be no doubt about his amazing gifts as a dancer nor of his major impact on the dance capitals of the world.

Choreographically he is difficult to assess. Diaghilev clearly had great faith in him and Diaghilev's judgement and ability to spot talent in the making was beyond question. Nijinsky's works were clearly ahead of his time and foreshadowed many of the later developments of modern barefoot dance in Germany and America yet his direct influence on these must at best be considered marginal. He had a great influence on his sister Bronislava Nijinska, a considerable choreographer in her own right. One of her most successful works, *Les Noces* to Stravinsky's music, would seem to embody all her brother's theories about dance and movement. She was never to do anything like it again. Even if Nijinsky's choreographic influence is confined to that one work, generally recognised as Nijinska's masterpiece, it would be enough to establish him in the ranks of outstanding creative makers of dance. Through the devoted adherence of Marie Rambert, his *L'Après Midi d'un Faune* survived more or less intact in performance and Rudolf Nureyev was happy to dance it in tribute to the master. Attempts have been made to reconstitute his *The Rite of Spring*, otherwise his creations have been lost.

It is remarkably appropriate that the role of Nijinsky in David Pownall's play should be performed by Nicholas Johnson. A distinguished dancer in his day, one of the few to make the transition from dance to straight acting, he is himself half Polish and speaks Polish fluently. He danced some of the leading roles as a principal with the Royal Ballet and then with London Festival Ballet, in a repertory of classics similar to those in which Nijinsky was trained and performed. Johnson himself danced Mercutio alongside Nureyev as Romeo in that choreographer's *Romeo and Juliet*. Nureyev's impact as a dancer is perhaps the only equivalent our generation has for the astonishing effect Nijinsky made in his own time. Johnson also performed the role of Nijinsky in the BBC Omnibus production *Nijinsky: God of the Dance*. He has shown in a wide variety of roles in the West End and on film that he can act as gracefully and as effectively as he used to dance.

Nicholas Dromgoole
London, 1997

NIJINSKY
DEATH OF A FAUN

The first production of *Nijinsky: Death of a Faun* took place at the Glynne Wickham Studio Theatre , Bristol University, on 23rd May 1991 with Nicholas Johnson as Nijinsky, directed by Jane McCullogh. The play has since been performed at the Edinburgh International Festival, and throughout the world including performances in Europe, Australia and the United States.

August 19th, 1920. Mid-morning

A basement in the Bellevue Sanatorium, Kreuzlingen, Switzerland with one upstage exit.

The pre-set dimly reveals a table and a straight-backed chair. To stage L are some cans of paint and a splattered dust-sheet beneath a pair of step-ladders.

NIJINSKY enters in a crumpled suit with a glass of tea in one hand and a case in the other.

He stands and waits for a moment, looking up blankly.

The lights go on.

He puts the glass of tea and the case on the table, then goes over and stares at the step-ladders.

Another light goes on.

He looks up angrily.

NIJINSKY

Make your mind up! How many lights am I allowed?

> *Pause. He returns to the table and takes a sip at his tea.*

Yesterday there was a telephone call from Venice.

It was for me, but Doctor Binswanger took it in his office because I am not allowed to receive uncensored news in case I react badly.

The most important phone call imaginable and I could not receive it directly. That is shameful.

They shame me, then they put it on the bill.

For receipt of tidings, X francs, account Nijinsky.

For passing on tidings, X francs, account Nijinsky.

>*He nods rhythmically as he repeats in monotone:-*

Account Nijinsky.

Account Nijinsky.

Account Nijinsky.

Account Nijinsky.

You know what it's like.

Hammering shame and you pay for it.

Yesterday there was a knock on the door.

I'm reading Tolstoy. I look up, "Enter!" I say.

In comes the Doctor, his glasses gleaming.

"I regret to tell you that your friend Diaghilev is dead."

He said it is was a thunderbolt to the psyche so I must be careful. How is one careful with a thunderbolt?

"Did you expect Diaghilev to die?," he said.

"Of course," I replied. "He was always abusing his body."

"No, I mean so soon. It was so unexpected."

So I told him: "Be more precise how you speak; that way you will run a better madhouse."

"Don't brood" was his final word.

I brooded, nonetheless. I brooded all night.

(*Urgently, nervously.*) I felt him! My soul was numb. Often he numbed my soul.

His thunderbolt was stuck in my numbness.

Sergei was everything. He did everything.

He took my wages. He took my time.

Sergei picked me up and put me on top of the Christmas tree.

Then he took me down off the top of the Christmas tree.

Whatever Sergei did to me, he did deliberately.

How do I know the telephone message was true?

Someone speaks into a machine and says "He's dead." That's not enough, not for him.

I must feel it. They tell me anything they like in this place.

> *Pause*

No, I must not lie to myself. I have seen it in the newspaper. Diaghilev is dead, in black and white.

He is dead and I am dead. We can be reunited.

I said: "I want to attend this funeral. I should be a pall-bearer. All of his old boy-friends should carry the coffin, if there's room."

Doctor Binswanger says no. It would do me no good. It would upset me.

"It's only death," I said. "Death doesn't frighten me."

"That's not why I'm against you going.

My objection is that the funeral would be too theatrical."

Well, he's supposed to be the expert.

> *Pause.*

Doctor Binswanger said he'd seen a funeral in Venice. The coffin goes on a black gondola to the island where the Venetians bury their dead.

I've been in a gondola with Sergei.

He has kissed me in a gondola.

That was a funeral in Venice.

> *Pause*

I told Doctor Binswanger that I must do something to show my respects.

Diaghilev had been the most important person in my life.

"Very well," he said. "You may have the sanatorium chapel to yourself for an hour or so; but you must behave in a decent manner."

> *A knocking sound is heard; five hammer blows from an adjoining room.*

A decent manner.

> *One blow.*

A decent manner.

> *Four blows.*

I am supposed to behave in a decent manner but Doctor Binswanger can continue to have his alterations done while I am meditating upon the passing of a world-famous impresario.

It would never occur to him to tell his builders to keep quiet while I am in contemplation of death and art and sorrow.

Progress is his god. He wants to be rich. He is rich! Extending his empire means a lot to him. Any grief of mine is a mere chore.

The knocking resumes for eight blows.

NIJINSKY sits on the chair, very still, blinking.

This sanatorium has grown year by year, so I'm told. Doctor Binswanger has got more and more popular with the insane. They flock to him from all over the world. And this place gets bigger and bigger!

I have to share my accommodation with all sorts.

The knocking resumes for three blows.

"Why don't you make friends with other people?" Doctor Binswanger says.

"Talk to them. Relate to them. They're just like you."

Like me? (*Stamps his foot.*) Like me? (*Stamps.*)

Like me? (*Stamps.*) Like me?

I thought we were all agreed that there's no one like me.

"Personality Uniqueness is a theory, but by no means proven."

So, we are all the same is the other theory

Pause.

I am Nijinsky.

No one else is Nijinsky.

Even my father was not Nijinsky.

He was Nijinsky's father.

Whatever happens, no matter how low I sink, how severe my humiliations,

I am always Nijinksy.

That's pride, a terrible thing—which you pretend not to understand.

But if you had been one of Doctor Binswanger's patients and he had been in the crowd at the Sermon on the Mount, he would have taken you aside afterwards and counselled you about self-love, and offered you a cure—at a price.

> *The knocking starts up again this time for ten blows.*

This will go on and on and on and on. Every day we feel it upstairs. The Doctor's alterations. Wait until they start drilling. People who are mad go even madder when they hear drilling under their pillows.

It is everyone's worst nightmare, the steel, the drill going into the brain.

Many of the patients are shell-shock cases from the war.

They hate the sound of machines.

I don't. I have no fear of that sound at all.

When I hear the drill I think of new movements.

I rise and twist, and twist and twist, a spiral, a thrusting spiralling move powering me upwards...

Impossible, of course.

I've tried it and almost broke my neck.

So, my philosophy is, do not try to beat the machine, enslave it.

Make a mechanical dancer who can do the drill.

He will have an advantage over other dancers.

No one will be able to torment his soul.

Doctor Binswanger assured me that this cellar is the inter-denominational sanatorium chapel. When I asked him whether he could swear that it is consecrated ground, he was evasive.

"Perhaps, at some time, it was," he mumbled. "I've heard it mentioned as a possible shrine hundreds of years ago to the patron saint of cheese-makers."

This was an obvious lie, something he had made up on the spot to keep me quiet. And when I asked the nurse who brought me down here if it was a sacred place he just laughed and said it was a sacred place if Doctor Binswanger said so because the Doctor paid his wages, but, as far as he knew, and he'd been working at the sanatorium since it opened, this sacred place used to be a storeroom, before that it was a porter's lodge, and before that a bakery.

So, I don't know what to believe. I've got a feeling that I've been fobbed off, but... if this is all there is...

"What sect are you?" Doctor Binswanger asked me. "Sect?" I said. "What do you mean, sect?"

"Are you Russian Orthodox?"

"Is that a sect?" I answered.

"Are you agnostic? Pagan? Deist? Mohammedan, perhaps?"

"I am a Polish Catholic." I told him proudly.

"Then here is your equipment," Doctor Binswanger said, putting this case in my hand. "Everything your sect requires is in there. Look after it well. Other patients

will need to use it after you. And leave the chapel as
tidy as you found it."

He opens the case. On top is a white cloth
which he takes out and examines.

Hm. Cotton: For Sergei? Cotton? Forgive me. Should
be silk.

He lays the cloth over the table but something
in the fall of the fabric through the air reminds
him of dance. He lays the cloth several times
smiling, enjoying the thought, exhilarated,
playing. Humming.

White for you, Sergei? White? (*Laughs.*) The husband
doesn't wear white. He's always in black, isn't he?

He finally leaves the cloth in place then takes
two candle-holders out of the case which he
puts on either side of the table, followed by
two candles which he sticks in the holders.

One for you, Sergei, and one for me. They've already
been used. I would have liked fresh candles for you,
virgin candles, but the Doctor has to save money.
(*Lights the candles.*) Flames. I love flames, Sergei. I
love the way they move through the air. Never the
same twice. Always new, always showing the way.

Often I model myself on a flame, wavering.

He takes a crucifix out of the case.

But you're just a piece of wood.

He puts the crucifix between the candles, steps
back, genuflects, then takes a packet of cigarettes
out of his pocket and lights one at a candle-
flame.

We're all set. This is now our cathedral, Sergei.
Coloured light streams through the stained-glass.

Imagine the organ. Imagine the incense. You've been lying in state in my mind since the news came through. God knows how many times I've queued up to walk round the open coffin and stare at your face. You have not changed.

> *He moves like a flame from one candle to another.*

I want to tell you that I love you you.

I want to tell you that I love you you.

I want to tell you that I love love love.

I want to tell you that I love love love.

I love but you do not. You do not love what He loves.

I love what He what He loves. You are death you are death.

I want to tell you that you are death, that you are death.

I want to tell you that you are death that you are death.

Death is death, but I am life.

I am life but you are death.

Defeat death by death by death.

You are death but I am life.

Defeat death by death by death.

I am death, but you are not life.

Life is life, and death is death.

You are death but I am life.

Defeat death by death by death.

I am death, but you are not life.

I want to tell you that you are death and I am life.

I want to tell you that I am life and you are death.

I love you my friend. I wish you good.

I wish you good, I love you you.

I wish you good. I do not wish you harm.

You do not love me you.

I love love you.

I wish you good.

I am yours and you are mine.

It's good that we are both dead

and can be together again.

He prays on his knees in front of the crucifix.

O God, whose nature it is ever to have mercy and to spare: we suppliantly entreat Thee on behalf of the soul of Thy servant whom Thou hast bid to pass out of this life; deliver him not, we beseech Thee, into the hands of the enemy, nor be Thou unmindful of him for ever...

Pause.

Before this room was a wood store, it was a porter's lodge.

Before it was a porter's lodge it was a bakery.

Before it was a bakery it was a railway station.

Before it was a railway station it was a place of exile for artistic Russian malefactors.

It has never been a sacred place, but it has a history.

Every space has a history. We can leave it at that.

The knocking starts again: Three loud knocks.

And that: (*One knock.*)

And that: (*One knock.*)

And that: (*Four knocks.*)

> *The knocking continues. He takes his jacket is off.*
>
> *Pause.*

He was knocking in a coffin nail. I'm surprised that I can hear it all the way from Venice but if we learn anything as we grow older it is that the world is shrinking, and when you're nailed up you can be sent anywhere.

> *More knocking —deadened—continues through...*

And the knocking, the knocking!

Everything is knocking into everything else.

(*Yells.*) Knock quieter, damn you!

> *Three loud knocks. Pause.*

Poor Sergei. What a body you had.

Crated up like a pile of costumes.

And to be despatched to Kreuzlingen!

Rome, Paris, New York, London, yes, but Kreuzlingen?

There's nothing here but me, waiting.

Waiting. Always waiting.

All those years of waiting.

What was I waiting for?

To be re-admitted to your love, Sergei?

To be taken back?

To be given my place at your side again?

What did I lose when you rejected me?

It's hardly worth thinking about.

I was merely the greatest dancer that the world had ever seen one day and nothing the next.

You did that with your magic wand.

Hey presto! "Now you see him, now you don't."

What power you people who can't dance have.

It is the artist's despair.

Which is something I am not permitted to think about or my condition will deteriorate at such speed that a sheet can make a rope and I'll find a place to tie it. I can jump. I've always been able to jump. In a few minutes it would all be over.

Pause.

"I am trusting you to behave sensibly, Herr Nijinsky," Doctor Binswanger said as I left his office. "Don't let me down."

Why shouldn't I let him down?

Unreasonable pain is for animals.

Animals don't know themselves. They have no soul.

I keep telling myself that I have only survived by descending to animalhood where art is meaningless.

When I wake up in the morning I feel myself and say:

"You're a bed-bug. Keep still and no one will squash you."

But the flesh still speaks.

Oh, my body is still Shakespeare.

It refuses to remain silent.

Always talking to me.

Lift yourself up!

Arise, O ye son of the morning!

But then comes the nurse with my injection.

The dance-killing injection.

The cloud that smothers the flame.

"Don't give it to me today," I begged.

"Not on the day of his funeral. I have to be myself."

"Fuck you," the nurse growled, and stuck it in my thigh.

This thigh.

This famous thigh.

And I felt the cloud that makes every day the same descending.

"No, no!" I cried, "go back! Get out of my blood!"

That's how I am.

I talk to the contents of syringes.

>   *Pause.*

But help came, Sergei. When the drug worked I didn't want to get up.

I wanted to lie there in the greyness but my body forced me out of bed. "Look! Look!" it said.

It's a good thing that I looked out of my window and saw the sight I saw:

Far away in a golden field

which had been scissored flat by the prudent Swiss,

there was a solitary black horse grazing the stubble.

The mountains watched him.

The sky watched him.

The universe watched him.

The angels in heaven watched him.

Every bird, every bee, every mouse, watched him.

It was all so still, so focussed.

Then the horse swished his tail and the landscape shook.

That is how you were once, my body said to me.

The centre of attention.

But now you need that horse's unselfconsciousness

and lack of vanity,

and if you dance today, master, it must be

as naturally as that horse walks,

an extension of your true animal ways.

By sheer willpower I then drove the drug into my bladder I chased it round my bloodstream until I had it cornered. Then I pissed it down the bowl and pulled the chain, saying: "Nijinsky will dance today!"

But I can't help being afraid.

Without the tranquiliser they say I'm in danger.

Odd how the fear is not unlike what I used to feel before going on-stage...

Oh, how I miss the dance! It is my whole life!

How could you take it away from me?

It would have been kinder to kill me!

No matter what wrong I had committed, that punishment was too great.

To close the theatres to me, to keep the people away!

Why didn't you come into our room one night and strangle me like Othello did Desdemona?

That would have been better for both of us.

But I can still dance.

Oh, yes. My body has not forgotten, even though I have often pleaded with it to do so.

The urge remains. The steps are imprinted.

Every move is history, taught by pain.

The last time I saw Sergei was seven months and twenty three days ago.

He took me to see Petrushka danced at the Paris Opera.

Why Petrushka?

Why did it have to be Petrushka?

All that trouble for me to see Petrushka. What for?

As if I didn't know! Ha! ...

It's his favourite.

> *He drops into a knock-kneed position, his arms hanging, his face pulled into a grotesque grimace.*

Whenever I danced Petrushka, that poor rag doll filled with straw, it aroused his lust.

He throws himself to the floor; makes several of Petrushka's movements.

All I ever had to do was drop into the role and Sergei would do anything for me.

"Do it. Do it! Do the rag doll! Please! Please!"

He dances, ending by the sheet. Kneeling, he puts it over his head.

Whenever I made up for Petrushka, Sergei came into my dressing room to watch. His eyes never left my face as I transformed myself into that wretched little creature.

Poor little Petrushka. In his box, his cell, his prison. Empty headed. A complete slave to the magician's whims, who had the key. But his spirit never died!

Throws off the sheet and leaps up.

Never died!

The rag doll lives!

He dances away ...

the rag doll lives! ...

...ending on the floor by the table. Pause, as he quietens and recovers.

Sergei could never be satisfied with even the lowest levels of my humiliations. Within my triumphs as Petrushka was this terrible knowledge gnawing at me, that it was, for him, a satanic pleasure to have me so belittled, so submissive, so pathetic. A man of straw, piece of wood, struggling to stay in one piece.

When he took me to see Petrushka again, he said:

"This will jolt you back to reality. You'll remember just how good you were as the rag-doll. The sweetness of your triumphs... which I arranged for you, my darling. Has there ever been such a Petrushka?

Watch them dance like you used to dance. It will bring it all back.

You will be resurrected. The present will cure the past."

He gets up.

"Do you feel guilty?" I asked, "Is that why you have brought me here?"

"Me? Ho-ho. Never. Hurry up, I haven't much time.

See, everyone is staring at you. They remember."

He enacts the following:

"Would you believe it?"

"It's Nijinsky!"

"What? Nijinsky? Surely not.

He can hardly climb the stairs.

His clothes are threadbare.

His eyes are dull.

What has happened to him?"

I watched Petrushka in my shame.

"Will you ever dance the rag doll again?" Sergei asked.

"The doll? The slave? The puppet?"

He spoke loudly so everyone could hear.

"Will you dance these parts again once Doctor Diaghilev has cured you with his shock tactics?"

Everyone watched to see if I would applaud the ballet.

Sits on chair.

I did but with one hand on my famous thigh, like this. (*Pats his thigh.*) So no one could see.

They were his dancers, his marionettes, my brothers and sisters in suffering, after all.

Then the old guard were all over me, laughing, feeling my muscles.

Enjoying my shame. Smoking their cigars and enjoying my shame.

Sergei loomed over me like a mountain.

"You must get yourself back in condition. You're being lazy, dear boy.

Come on, Vatsa. You must dance for me again."

I told him that I would never dance again.

That hurt him. His eyes bled.

"Oh, Vatsa, my darling, did I do this to you?"

"Yes," I told him, "I will never dance again... except on your grave."

The knocking starts up again: Five blows.

Except on your grave!

Knocking: Three blows.

Except on your grave!

Knocking: Three blows.

Nijinsky copies the knocking.

Except on your grave!

Except on your gra-a-a-a-a-ave!

Pause. He laughs. He drinks.

Pause. He looks at his watch.

I am already late for the funeral. He died yesterday.

I must ask the Virgin to intercede on his behalf with the supreme judge. Let him off a thousand years of Purgatory.

Well, five hundred.

He should get five hundred thousand if there's any justice.

Which is a big IF.

How can I pray for Sergei in a place like this? It's so ugly!

To pray for Sergei I need to be somewhere beautiful.

Sergei will supervise his own funeral.

See that everything is properly organised—that all the tickets are sold, the costumes right, talent breathing, genius appreciated and cherished.

And there should be music.

In a real chapel it would be organ music.

You can't dance to organ music.

It has no sense of humour. No one can dance without that.

I have a sense of humour.

Sergei will have music for his funeral. It won't be Stravinsky.

Who could get buried to Stravinsky? (*He dances.*)

Debussy! Now there's a spirit! (*He dances again.*)

Let him have Debussy for his funeral. (*Little dance.*)
Let the vibrations be so intense that they make waves
for the gondola. Let there be a disaster. Let his body
be lost, like mine.

Sergei even instructed his manservant:

"Keep your eye on Nijinsky. Watch him wherever
he goes. Take the name of any man or woman he
talks to. He belongs to me.

Every step he takes is mine.

Every breath he breathes is mine.

He was nothing. A plaything for rich men.

A dog. A hungry dog." (*Pause.*)

"Vatsa, my dear boy, love me, love me.

You have often been a dog.

Now I want you to be another animal."

"What animal?" I said. "Tell me. I'll do any animal
you like."

"Can you manage a faun?"

"You mean a young boy deer?"

"No, not a young boy deer, dear boy, a young half-
man half-goat."

"Not a simple matter. What does a faun do? How
does it go?"

"A faun throbs."

"Say again?"

"It grows. It grows horns. It grows up. No, this is not
for bed. It's for ballet. You must read Stephen
Mallarmé's *l'après midi d'un faune*," he said. "Sublime,"
he said.

"With Debussy," he said.

"So evocative of our Greek days together. Awakening desire is the theme," he said.

A throbbing half-man half-goat growing horns and up!

The things they ask dancers to do.

"Where will I find an animal to base it on," I asked. "There are no half-men half-goats in the zoo."

He took me to a goat-farm on the Black Mountain and left me.

I watched the young bucks in rut very closely.

From what I could tell they looked so, stood so, moved so.

"Very good," Sergei said when I showed him on his return. "You've got it exactly."

Then I showed him how the young bucks

piss on each other's heads

to liberate strong-smelling secretions

from sex-glands on the forehead;

how they can copulate ten times

in ten minutes;

how they greedily gobble up the shit of the females.

"The audience won't need any of that," Sergei said. "You stick to a few simple movements."

"But that will only be half the truth," I complained.

"You are only playing half a goat," he replied, and took me away.

As I worked on the choreography for *l'après midi d'un faune* I became suspicious of his motives.

Why ask me to do this *now*?

Having put half the truth of the goat into the dance

I realised that only half the truth of the man would fit it.

Which half did he want?

I asked Sergei what part of me he wanted on the stage.

"The part that yearns for a natural mate," he told me.

There was a cool look in his eyes.

Rain came down from the Black Mountain, filling my heart.

"Who is looking for a mate?" I said.

"You should be," he replied, "but only find one who will understand that I can never completely let you go."

I am always smiling.

Doctor Binswanger says it would be better if I didn't smile all the time. Just some of the time when the occasion calls for it.

But I am not smiling.

> *Runs around stage...*

I am snarling, snarling, snarling.

> *Puts on jacket: sits on stool, head on knees.*

In the old days, all I cared about was my body.

I used to examine it closely. (*Stands on stool.*)

I held mirrors to see parts which were normally invisible.

I even stood on mirrors for unusual perspectives.

I worshipped my body (*To crucifix.*) as Christians worship yours.

Everyone said: "Look after your body, Vatsa, and it will look after you."

Now I don't care about my body very much.

But I care about what goes on in my head, where my dancing is done now that I'm dead.

> *Jumps down off the stool.*

It's a great relief once you're dead.

You don't have to worry about dying, for a start.

What are the dead but fragments of themselves?

People in pieces. People melting.

People decomposing into separate parts.

There are patients in this sanatorium who are divided between two natures.

They have two personalities; two ways of looking at things.

But I can beat that. In my madness.

On Monday I was God the father.

Tuesday, God the Son.

Wednesday, God the Holy Ghost.

Thursday, Tolstoy.

Friday, God the all-seeing.

Saturday, God half asleep.

On Sunday I was God the audience.

That's seven personalities which must be a record.

I'm glad I cured myself of thinking I was seven gods.

It's helped me, leaving all that baggage behind.

My madness, such as it is, seems to be limited these days to talking to myself, but, when I've got nothing to say I keep quiet which is an attitude that a lot of talkative people could learn from.

As for being withdrawn, well, there was a lot of pain which I didn't want to encounter again.

My wife has stuck me in here while she goes to America to lecture on how I used to dance. Sad, but we need the money.

The American government would not give me permission to enter the country. The American government does not allow mentally unsound people to enter the country. We need the money to keep me in here.

I am not mentally unsound. I am not my wife. I can dance,

I can lecture on dancing. I can earn money to keep me in here.

But I cannot lecture on how I *used* to dance. That is too sad.

My wife has left me here in this sanatorium. I will never get out.

My wife should be here in this sanatorium and I should be in America lecturing on dancing. My wife is a terrible dancer. Always was.

Doctor Binswanger says that there's money to be made in America.

The Stock Exchange on Wall Street is going mad but they are making money. I am mad but I am not making any money, stuck here.

My wife is afraid of poverty.

Today there is no god. There is only a piece of wood.

Piece of Wood, I intercede for Sergei Pavlovich Diaghilev

He is not a villain for all time.

Just for the time he was with me.

I am Nijinsky, the leaper.

I leapt into bed with Prince Pavel Dmitrievich Lvov who passed me on to Sergei Pavlovich Diaghilev who passed me on to madness.

When madness tires of me he will pass me on to Tolstoy because Tolstoy has all the answers. Good old Tolstoy.

I am not permitted to read his books. *War and Peace* upset me.

I thought that was the idea.

Tolstoy knows nothing of poverty.

He gambles on the Stock Exchange but he writes well.

My wife comes from an aristocratic background.

She could lecture on flower arrangement but not dancing.

I am the dancer. I am the leaper. I am Nijinsky.

Stalin will go to Sergei Pavlovich Diaghilev's funeral.

He will torpedo the gondola.

He will give a funeral oration about collectivisation over the wreckage.

Stalin gambles on the Stock Exchange.

He is an American pretending to be a Russian.

I am a Russian. No, I'm not.

I am a Pole pretending to be a Russian but I do not gamble on the Stock Exchange.

I am in the storeroom with the wood. The Piece of Wood.

The wood is my only salvation. The piece of it.

So, we'll wait for Sergei together.

It may take some time for him to arrive. Paddling a heavy black gondola all the way from Venice, under the Alps, is a long business.

All his old boy-friends will be having a roaring party under the mountains, tap dancing on the coffin, drinking pink champagne by torchlight, boogy-woogying to Debussy, and he will be lying there, his great head contemplating our reunion.

What thoughts will he have? Guilt, certainly.

Not about my suffering but what he did to the civilised world by crippling ME; its greatest creator of the dancer's art... by deliberately... wilfully... murdering genius... starving me... pushing me away... ruining my life.

> *Throws jacket on floor.*
>
> *Pause.*
>
> *Sits on chair (reversed).*
>
> *His head drops.*
>
> *He looks up.*

I am insane.

No one who was sane would have such dreams.

I am nothing. I have no power over myself.

Who am I when no one is applauding?

A loosened piece of nonsense.

But I see things that are true. Even Doctor Binswanger has to admit that I can be inspired. He confided to me one day

"Don't tell a soul that I said this, but I envy you those disturbing fantasies of mind. They are beautiful, beautiful in the way you used to dance.

I saw you perform once in Paris, '*Le Spectre de la Rose*', and as I talk to you now In your great sickness of soul, I realise that you are still dancing, still leaping, still astonishing even yourself.

Look upon your agony of mind as a blessing. When It is over count It as yet another creative period.

No mind is in perfect balance.

Nothing is still, nothing is constant. We shift like sand under the sea.

Your mind is as good as anyone else's, my dear mad Vatsa".

> *Pause.*

Such comfort. Such comfort.

What is there to cling on to if you're extraordinary and suffering, but ordinariness? Even that he takes away from me.

(*To crucifix.*) You had a crown of thorns, mine is atoms, scatterings, all whirling, pointless, buzzing around my brain. Destiny has gone. Direction has disappeared.

All the dancing masters are dead.

Pause.

It Is very depressing.

I am a man of form and I live in a world becoming more and more formless. Doctor Binswanger will not even argue with me any more. He tries to be light-hearted to lift my spirits, but I resist in case it goes on the bill.

If you leap, leap from one side of your mind to the other.

Stay in those limits. Let that be your stage.

There are steps I have invented which will revolutionise the dance. Only I can do them.

There is this-one.

He moves his head sharply.

To an outsider, and out of context, it may look like nothing, but you understand it, Piece of Wood.

Repeats the jerk of the head.

Turning away the face.

Face to the wall. The loneliness.

And this one.

He folds himself slowly into a foetus position on the floor.

Growing backwards. Climbing back into the beginning.

I have thousands of new moves. We will never discover them all.

But the ones which rule the ballet as it is today are based on the crumbling postures of aristocrats.

Jerks his head.

I say that to it. Face to the wall.

Pause.

We are in bondage to stories, you and I.

No one has ever got your story right, and no one will ever get mine. Mine will be in Dr Binswanger's file, yours in the dust of Jerusalem. The stories of my new ballets were primitive. They were about sex and power, not rubbish like *'Le Spectre de la Rose'*, romantic twaddle. Mine are from Tolstoy and very realistic.

In my new choreography no one ever dances on the points of their toes because that is all over.

They stand flat-footed, an extension of the earth, and when they move it is like a worker or a farmer doing something eternal.

A pneumatic drill starts up and the light flicker.

He convulses, holding his head.

The drilling stops.

A spasm.

There is no movement more fundamental.

In birth, in human love, or death, it is spasm, spasm, spasm, not pirouette.

If you want to change things, you're dangerous. You know that!

You were a new sort of god. I was a new sort of artist.

Both of us had to be put away, so the old, blind madness could continue to be king.

If you could have heard that audience on the opening night of my new ballet, '*The Sacred Rites of Spring*', you would have heard the bloodthirsty cries of the Jews when they bayed for your life and let Barabbas go. They hated it.

Show us the boys and girls, the beautiful bodies, but keep your spasms to yourself, Nijinsky. Well, they got their way.

I am here,

alone with my spasms,

surrounded by other people's spasms,

with no spotlight on mine,

and no applause,

except that which comes at the end of my wife's lectures

about me

and how I used to dance,

far away, unheard, unseen,

in a distant land.

I wish I could hear it

even though it is applause for a dead man.

I wish I could hear it

even though the money she earns

is to keep me in prison.

I wish I could hear it

because it is mine!

He bows and bows as if taking curtain calls.

I have done what was required of me by my inner power.

There is no need for me to be ashamed.

Dance shoots out with the baby in a costume of blood,

never still, never still....

> *Runs his fingers down the figure on the crucifix.*

Never still. Never still. Nothing is ever still.

When I first saw you on the cross, I was a very small boy, in church.

I thought, in my innocence, that you were simply a dancer,

yes, a dancer jumping, your feet crossed in an *entrechat,*

and you were held there at the high point before you could come down.

My father bowed to you. My mother bowed to you.

Everyone who came in to the church bowed to you.

To a dancer.

"Who is that performer?" I asked,

"That is God," my father told me, "in his final agony."

"Will he ever come down?" I said.

My father told me not to ask stupid questions.

But every time I have seen your image since, it has been as a dancer first and God second.

There was a time when I was so hurt I thought I was you.

But now I don't think I'm God any more.

I simply don't want the job.

Doctor Binswanger can be God if he likes. To stop people smiling is the work of God.

Stravinsky makes them deaf, Tolstoy puts their eyes out, Stalin blows their heads off, and I'm the article stored in the storeroom

waiting for someone to find a use for me.

Let them pity me.

I am Nijinsky, the leaper.

Where is my leap now?

It is here. It is the reason I am here.

My leap is the telephone call which came across the Alps from Venice to tell me Diaghilev is dead.

He's dead! I'm so happy!

> *Does a few waltz steps, humming a melody from* The Sleeping Beauty.
>
> *Then plunges into gloom, very still.*
>
> *Pause.*

Every woman wanted me. I struck at the core. They couldn't help it.

It was ceaseless desiring, following, asking, begging, sending notes,

crying, wanting to be joined with Nijinsky.

I got very bored with it all and went to prostitutes because they couldn't care less who I was as long as I paid up.

That I found very refreshing.

They didn't talk about me.

They didn't exchange notes.

I was in and out and away on the wind.

But the others, the ladies ...

They wanted my scalp at their belts.

Why? To laugh and say: "He's nothing, really. It's all a dream."

I heard that some of them bet each other that they could have me.

Did you mind, Sergei? I know that sometimes you set these women onto me. Why did you do that? Why play the pimp? Because they had influence? (*Furiously.*) The body and the mind are connected, you know! (*Pause.*) How did I dance through all that pollution and treachery? It can only have been an inner hope for purity some day. So who was he? Ooo iz 'ee, this Prince Igor? All this female adoration! It made me glow but emptily. I worshipped my body as much as they did but the time came when I knew that I must escape from Sergei and find some respect.

I was on a ship. The clear, simple sea was all around me as we forged ahead. Get married, I thought. That's the way to do it. Who to? Ah, there's a woman leaning over the rail, watching me. She'll do. She'd been watching me for years, one of the thousands. I wrote her a note. Would you like to get married? She pounced. I fell back, a wedding at my throat. I had moved too soon.

I was drunk with freedom, alone on the ocean without Sergei breathing down my neck and I did not know what I was losing.

Losing, losing, losing; you know all about losing.

They must have made you dance that day.

Pains in your feet, pains in your hands, pains in your side,

a dancer's day, on the bar.

And the soldiers held their shields up as mirrors

so you could see how correct your dancing was

according to the master.

> *He does a little dance before the crucifix.*

> *Then takes it off the table and climbs up the step-ladders with it to the top, singing.*

I'm the Devil, tempting you on that high place.

If you do as I say then I'll give you the world.

If you do as I say you can have what you want.

No? You're turning down my wonderful offer?

If you're as good as you say you are, then throw yourself off and we'll see who saves you from being squashed on the rocks below!

See what I mean?

He's a fraud.

Jesus didn't jump because he wouldn't please the Devil,

but I did!

> *He jumps down with the crucifix held over his head like a boy with a toy aeroplane, then tears round the stage making engine noises, swooping and diving.*

Rat-tat-tat-tat! Rat-tat-tat-tat!

Down in flames I go! Blasted to bits!

He hurls the crucifix across the stage.

He stops, horrified.

God forgive me.

What have I done?

He picks the crucifix up and examines it.

No harm done.

He puts the crucifix back on the table and genuflects.

Sorry.

Sorry, Piece of Wood.

I got carried away.

I should tell Doctor Binswanger what I did so he can put it in his file on me.

"Threw God across the room."

'Motivation?"

"Frustration!"

He will write an article: "Projections of Religious Delusion" and get a lot of money for it.

Doctor Binswanger will find out what I've done down here.

He'll be told that I've committed sacrilege.

"How do you excuse that, Herr Nijinsky?' he'll say.

"I was seeking perfection," is always my answer.

"Through my body which is my prison." Stupid man!

He kicks over stool and chair.

Violent acts! Violent acts!

I am a violent man, at heart, but all dancers are violent. They have to be or they would never move a muscle.

Audiences expect them to be violent.

Ordinary people sit in chairs or walk up and down the street

but dancers rage in frenzies on and off the stage.

When you hear them talk, all that treacle, that's just to stop them hitting each other long enough to get the work done.

I had many enemies, I've punched people in my time.

And you, if I remember, withered the fig tree for not having any fruit,

and beat up the money changers.

They were both aggressive acts which would have interested Doctor Binswanger.

But my violence, like yours, comes from frustration

when I'm not getting anywhere,

when I can see my goal and everyone is holding me back.

> *Pause.He picks up the stool, then the chair,
> which he turns and sits on, reversed.*
>
> *Takes off tie.*

When Diaghilev cast me aside it was not because I had married a woman in defiance of his wishes, as was rumoured, but for something much worse:

I was about to eclipse him.

My moment of Infallibility was imminent.

And he remained stuck in his sins, envy and spite, wanting me to fall, yearning for my breakdown.

Crossing himself.

Why has thou forsaken me? Why has thou forsaken me?

We are brothers, and we have suffered the same.

Yes, and the public adored us both.

Why did they adore me?

That man Nijinsky can do the impossible.

He can work miracles with his body.

Have you witnessed his leaping and dancing?

With it he can cure the sick, open the eyes of the blind,

drive away despair, bring light into darkness,

raise Lazarus from his ennui!

How does he do it?

What is his secret?

A foot.

Just a foot.

Look at this foot.

He wiggles his toes.

As ugly as any other. Not spring-loaded. No ankle-wings like Mercury

A simple foot, just bone and gristle like anyone else's.

They said that when I leapt, I rose in the air to an

unbelievable height, then floated back to the ground like thistledown.

I defied gravity. All from this smelly foot.

And the nails driven into it by Diaghilev,

damn him!

And that's how you leapt up.

That's how you rose from the dead. From the foot.

And I will be resurrected from the foot when that lecher comes to nail me for the last time all the way from Venice.

Then I will be released from death to dance in the universe.

That's why he has to come in his black gondola and take me with him.

He is my true mate.

He is the man to my goat, and the goat to my man.

He is my *l'après midi*. He is my awakening, always.

While I've been in here I've been working on a ballet about strong sexual feelings.

I want to show the outpouring from the inner source, the fountain.

The main thing about my ballet is that it has to be completely honest.

Nothing is to be excluded.

Half-measures are out.

The mind would open up and reveal all its treasures if it went on.

All disgust would be banished.

That is the true stuff of dance. To abolish disgust.

The courage to show the impulses with grace but not disguise.

Like those goats on the Black Mountain in their frenzy, their freely-flowing frenzy.

My ballet is here in my notebook.

It can only be finished when Sergei comes back to me.

A week will be needed to perform it, like Wagner's *Ring*.

Whoever thought that life only takes a couple of hours to perform?

It takes at least a week to do the cycle.

Lust is the subject.

Not love.

I tried to make this ballet before—when I was out in the world, free!

It was a failure because I was in the aftermath of a great hurt.

Diaghilev had told me that he wanted to have two boys.

Me and someone else.

So I put together a ballet called *Jeux! Jeux!* Oh, *Jeux!*

It was not a success. I did not feel it, this *Jeux!*

Three young men are lusting. Two of them are camouflaged as girls.

It was the life of which Diaghilev dreamt. I did it to please him.

A tennis game of nets and rackets and lines—Love-all!

Love-fifteen! Love-thirty! Love-forty!

Love as many as you lust after!

I wanted people to feel disgust!

But I didn't mean it. Love is sacred. Lust is just creation.

Madness is not being able to help telling the whole truth.

The whole body, the whole spirit.

The bucks helping each other by pissing on their foreheads

to make lust to make love.

Sergei only wanted things by halves.

Which is art.

And God the Creator

has been trying to piss on artists' foreheads since time began,

but they keep running away and hiding in Diaghilev's theatres.

If that great impresario had spotted your talent, half-man, half-god, you know the half he would have wanted.

He is the most blasphemous of men

because all he loves is beauty,

and beauty is not always divine.

They said my faun was obscene.

They did not notice that my Jeux was actually obscene.

They just paid for their tickets, watched the movements,

then went home uncomprehendingly.

I have been dead many times.

The first was in Paris when I had typhoid fever.

I noticed the doctor and Diaghilev exchanging glances.

They understood without words.

I also understood without words.

The doctor left the room and Diaghilev made me an offer.

I was in a fever, but alive.

I accepted the offer and I died for the first time.

I was twenty years old.

I had been frightened of life.

I knew that my mother had been frightened of life and I had inherited this weakness from her.

I did not want to agree.

Diaghilev sat on my bed and insisted.

He inspired me with fear. I wept and wept.

I understood death.

I could not run away.

I was eating an orange.

I was thirsty and had asked Diaghilev for an orange.

I must have fallen asleep with the orange in my hand because when I woke up the orange was all squashed and lying on the floor.

Then I realised that he had taken it from my hand while I was asleep

and stamped on it.

He will be here soon.

There is another death I will have to die.

I have sworn an oath that I will not dance again except on his grave.

This is his grave.

Kneels.

This is his grave, where I am.

It has been dug for him, by me.

Today is the day of his funeral but he has not yet been brought on the black gondola, his catafalque streaming with ribbons, his corpse's face white as a clown's,

We must wait.

Let us be silent, and listen for Sergei coming.

Pause.

Nothing. Nothing keeps happening.

Sergei's playing with me, making me wait.

Never mind. I can hear the music. I'll work on my ballet.

I'm choreographing it right now in my head.

My scheme for annotating movement is still as valid as the day I hit upon it.

It's going through my brain.

Foot. Foot. Hand. Hand. Arm. Arm. Leg. Leg. Torso. Torso. Torso. Torso.

> *The pneumatic drill starts again.*
>
> *The lights flicker and dim.*
>
> *The drilling stops.*

Sergei is that you, darling? What an entrance!

The black gondola has come clean through the wall and shed its load.

The body shakes in its coffin.

Flakes of powder fall from the waxy cheeks and one eyelid trembles.

You know that you have arrived at your tomb, Sergei?

Bless you for coming.

> *A very heavy, thunderous blow from the next room.*
>
> *Lights flicker and go off.*

Thunderbolt.

> *Another very heavy blow from the next room.*
>
> *The lights flicker and come on even dimmer than before.*

Darling, darling Sergei, driving into my flesh again in darkness.

As usual, your entrance is powerful, sweeping everything aside and you say nothing in deference to my feelings as you desecrate my body.

> *Pause*

I take note of the respectful silence of the boy-friends who lie along the sides of the gondola, exhausted, knowing that the scene has changed. This is THE boy-friend.

Their dancing—that trivial stuff—is over.

The real show is about to begin.

It is time for me to fulfill my promise to dance again for you,

but it cannot be on your grave

because I am in it.

We are in it together, at last. Both dead, both buried.

> *Pause.*

> *Lights have dimmed to single spot on him.*

I smell your perfume. Musk. Musk.

Secreted by a male deer, dear male.

> *Another heavy blow.*

> *The lights come back on; brighter than original state.*

> *He falls back on the floor.*

What a crowd! All to see the show. Everybody's here!

A day to remember, Sergei. Jerusalem has never seen the like.

> *He lies flat on the floor, arms outstretched, upper torso slightly raised.*

From down here I recognise familiar faces as I look up:

teachers, friends, lovers, apostles, dancing partners,

oh, the helmet suits you, Sergei, and the style with which you pose with that hammer!

Such nonchalance! Such elan!

The audience quietens down. A hush.

That magic moment as the curtain rises to reveal the scene.

The hammering starts again.

Right hand! O suffering God!

He convulses with pain, screaming.

Left hand! Have mercy, darling Sergei!

Cross your feet, malefactor!

He screams again, writhing over the hammering.

All the way through both feet with a long, long nail!

The hammering continues.

No more! No more! No more! No more!

Pity me.

The hammering stops with a couple of louder blows.

He is absolutely flat on the floor.

He twists and turns with his hands and feet fixed in the points of crucifixion.

Unthinkable pain, Sergei. Unthinkable dancing.

Now, as you can see, I am stuck in this *entrechat.*

There is no one to lift me up so everyone can see me.

So I can hang.

Will you lift me up? Will you raise me?

You lifted me up once, hung me up before the whole adoring world,

then sent me to Hell.

> *He bends his knees and brings himself forward,*
> *then gets to his feet, his arms still outstretched.*

Careful Sergei! The god of the dance is in your hands.

Don't let the nails tear out or we'll have to do it all over again.

So, scene the first: the crucifixion.

It went well, I thought.

The second scene is mental. It takes place in the thoughts.

The spirit frees itself from the nails by an act of sheer self-discipline. I rip myself away from the cross.

Tear! Tear! Tear!

Blood flying everywhere!

> *He yanks himself free from the imaginary cross*
> *and dances away.*

Now I'll dance your way, Sergei, no more spasms, no more pain.

The old style, the old feeling.

The exquisite torture of *Scheherazade!*

> *Dances.*

Slushy, sentimental *Sylphides!*

> *Dances.*

The bloody *Spectre de le Rose!*

Dances.

Albrecht dancing to stay alive!

Dances.

*Suddenly he snaps into the grotesque position
of the puppet, Petrushka, hanging on the wall
like a broken man on the cross.*

Sorry to go back to this, Sergei.

But you'll understand by now, I'm sure.

This is my favourite role. Is it still yours?

The crucifixion of *Petrushka*.

Hanging here like this one has time to think before
the curtain goes up.

What's happened to me?

What have I done wrong?

Who am I?

Where am I going?

To be unknown, forgotten and unfulfilled all at the
same time

Is a great achievement, even for a man of straw.

They called me the god of the dance,

A title which no one can take away from me.

Pause.

Come on, Magician Sergei, touch me with your wand
once more.

Bring me to life.

Ah, your touch!

He starts to dance the role of Petrushka.

What a gift you have given me.

Life! Life!

He stops.

The wooden-headed puppet has been disobedient.

He must be punished, rejected, spurned, then cast aside, unwanted.

He dances the defiant finale, ending up on the floor, breathing hard.

Can't take it any more.

Not up to it.

Out of training, you understand.

Too much sitting, Sergei.

Ten years of sitting.

Sitting

and staring

sitting and staring

sitting and staring and smiling at nothing

Face to the wall.

He jerks his head.

You remember?

One of my new moves.

Face to the wall.

Things will get quieter now.

I've done a lot of talking today.

I've come back to life for a while, for a spasm.

That was in your honour, Sergei, in your honour.

Let it be said:

You made me.

Perhaps you had the right to break me.

>*He blows out the candles.*
>
>*Blackout.*

THE END